Words of poetry for:

Introduction

What springs to mind when you think about the natural world? Plants and animals? Weather and landscapes? Humans? As these poems show, nature is by no means a fixed thing with a simple definition. It's better understood as a kaleidoscope of different pieces, constantly shifting depending on who is looking.

Poetry can breathe life into the parts of our Earth that may not spark our interest at first glance. Do you think people would be more likely to protect moss if they saw it as a "blessing on the forest"? Would they look differently at a river if they could imagine its flowing as a "square-dance with boulders"?

The poems in this collection allow us to peer into the kaleidoscope and see familiar things in new ways: fading daylight becomes the "shadowy veil between light and dark", the forest turns into a "bad dream woman" and the otter is an "underwater thunderbolter"! We hope that these poems kindle your imagination and expand your own world.

LITTLE TIGER
LONDON

Contents

I Wonder

Does a butterfly miss
its wiggly caterpillar days?

Do tadpoles suspect
that they'll soon grow four
jumpy legs?

How does the leafy future
of an immense green tree
fit inside this tiny
seed?

I don't know, but I'm going to plant
many seedlings anyway, so that by the time
I'm old, a whole forest will wave
happy branches.

Margarita Engle

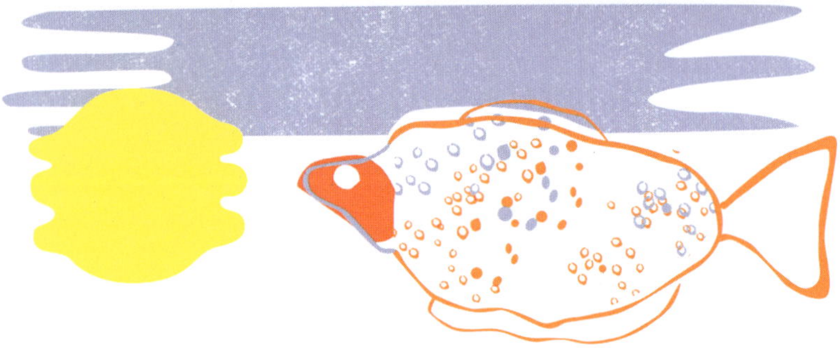

What Is the Pond Doing?

(for Ruairidh, who asked)

Wobbling like a wobbly jelly
Being a bucket for the rain
Sending flash-backs to the sun
Cheeking the sky
Giving the moon a bath
Letting swans, ducks and winter leaves ride on its back
Licking the lollipop reeds
Pretending to be soup for the wind to stir
Growing stinky skunk cabbages
Drawing wheels and circles then rubbing them out
Plopping slopping slurping spinning
Turning the weeping willows happily upside down
Dreaming of running away to sea
Hiding under a starry blanket of dark

What is the pond doing?
Ponding. Responding.

Diana Hendry

9

For Forest

Forest could keep secrets
Forest could keep secrets

Forest tune in every day
to watersound and birdsound
Forest letting her hair down
to the teeming creeping of her forest-ground

But Forest don't broadcast her business
no Forest cover her business down
from sky and fast-eye sun
and when night come
and darkness wrap her like a gown
Forest is a bad dream woman

Forest dreaming about mountain
and when earth was young
Forest dreaming of the caress of gold
Forest roosting with mysterious eldorado

and when howler monkey
wake her up with howl
Forest just stretch and stir
to a new day of sound

but coming back to secrets
Forest could keep secrets
Forest could keep secrets
And we must keep Forest

Grace Nichols

Otter

Otter enters river without falter – what a
supple slider out of holt and into water!

This shape-shifter's a sheer breath-taker, a
sure heart-stopper – but you'll only ever spot
a shadow-flutter, bubble-skein, and never
(almost never) actual otter.

This swift swimmer's a silver-miner – with
trout its ore it bores each black pool deep
and deeper, delves up-current steep and
steeper, turns the water inside-out, then
inside-outer.

Ever dreamed of being otter? That
utter underwater thunderbolter, that
shimmering twister?

Run to the riverbank, otter-dreamer, slip
your skin and change your matter, pour
your outer being into otter – and enter
now as otter without falter into water.

Robert Macfarlane

Mud

It's all over my wellies,
And there's specks all down my coat.
Teacher says it looks like
We've been swimming in a moat.

We were serving up mud pies,
And a splat got on my shirt.
Digging with our fingers,
Now we're head to toe in dirt.

Jumping in the puddles
And dancing in the rain –
Dad says he hopes the washing
Doesn't clog the drain.

The grown-ups don't like mud
But it's where the seed's first sown.
It's where the wriggly worms
Like to make their home.

So, though I'm sorry for the mess,
You really ought to know
We should all be thankful
For the things that help us grow.

Ruth Awolola

Little Blanco River

You're only a foot deep
under green water
your smooth shale skull
is slick & cool
blue dragonfly
skims you like a stone
skipping   skipping
it never goes under
you square-dance with boulders
make a clean swishing sound
centuries of skirts
lifting & falling
in delicate rounds
no one makes a state park out of you
you're not deep enough
little blanco river
don't ever get too big

Naomi Shihab Nye

Duskingtide

somewhere
between
  the last second of day
  first second of night
between
  the daily swap
  of sun and moon

that shadowy veil between
light and dark vanishes in

a wizardly puff

the world is now bewitched
spellbound inside and out

forests are frosted in silver-leafed sleep

fiery red clouds harden into
  black-browed mountains
  clamorous sky creatures

a thousand lost spirits
are set loose in spectral air swirls

bouquets of buried stars
out-pop through purple sky-fields

telltale scents
twine round the low-flying moon

twilight's small sounds
amplify into a chorus of giants

till the deep loud duskingtide
this ancient gloaming
this breathless semi-dark
spins
in one incandescence
into pure night

and with just a
tiny candle-strike

is gone

Zaro Weil

In Praise Of

Imagine moss.
It is a blessing on the forest.
It is green and green and green.

Rain falls and makes the river a poem
in praise of moss, which grows
and knows the old ways, like folklore.

Imagine speaking green to the forest
floor, living fatherless, flowerless, flowering
rootless, reaching deep into things.

Imagine moss, which feeds no one.
Which holds water like a breath.
Which blesses shade.

So let your life run through you
like new growth, which stores light, which lets go
of each clean breath joyfully,

which survives, which heals
wounds, which stands against fire
and is so green, like the river,

a blessing on the forest.

Rachel Plummer

The Mollusk That Made You

Shell of the sunrise,
sunrise shell,
yours is the pink lip
of a pearled world.

Who swirled your whorls and ridges?
Was it the shy gray wizard
shuttered inside you?
I hear he walks on one foot
and wears a magic mantle,
trailing stars.

O Shell,
if only I could shrink!
I'd climb your bristled back,
slide down the spiral
    of your heart.
I'd knock on your tiny door
    and ask to meet
    the mollusk
    that made you.

Joyce Sidman

Your Dresses

I like your rain dress,
its strange, sad colour,
its small buttons like tears.

I like your fog dress,
how it swirls around you
when you dance on the lawn.

23

Your snow dress I like,
its million snowflakes
sewn together with a needle of ice.

But I love your thunderstorm dress,
its huge, dark petticoats,
its silver stitches flashing as you run away.

Carol Ann Duffy

The Average Hippopotamus

The average hippopotamus
is big from top to bottomus,
it travels at a trotamus,
and swims when days are hotamus.
Because it eats a lotamus,
it's practically a yachtamus,
so it's a cinch to spotamus
the average hippopotamus.

Jack Prelutsky

To Make a Garden

To make a garden all you need
Is just a single simple seed,
A patch of earth, a sheltered spot
That's not too cold, but not too hot,
A little rain, a lot of sun,
That's all you need;
And when you're done,
In some strange way your seed will know
Just how to sprout and how to grow
Until you see to your surprise
A miracle before your eyes,
A baby leaf still curled up tight
That's pushing upward toward the light.
What will it be? A tree? A weed?
Each one is started from a seed.

Mary Ann Hoberman

Winter Poem

once a snowflake fell
on my brow and i loved
it so much and i kissed
it and it was happy and called its cousins
and brothers and a web
of snow engulfed me then
i reached to love them all
and i squeezed them and they became
a spring rain and i stood perfectly
still and was a flower

Nikki Giovanni

Colouring In

And staying inside the lines
Is fine, but...
I like it when stuff leaks –
When the blue bird and the blue sky
Are just one blur of blue flying,
And the feeling of the feathers in the air
And the wind along the blade of wing
Is a long gash of smudgy colour.
I like it when the flowers and the sunshine
Puddle red and yellow into orange,
The way the hot sun on my back
Lulls me – muddles me – sleepy
In the scented garden,
Makes me part of the picture...
Part of the place.

Jan Dean

Dear Stegosaurus

Bus-sized and gentle, you are master of peace,
diplomacy, berries, grass, perseverance, pace.

Your warm, rough belly sags with majesty over ferns,
cycads and dust. Your spikes are dull and magnificent,

a row of abandoned kites, rusted by a tough winter,
in a tree stripped of guts. You're not a fighter, though

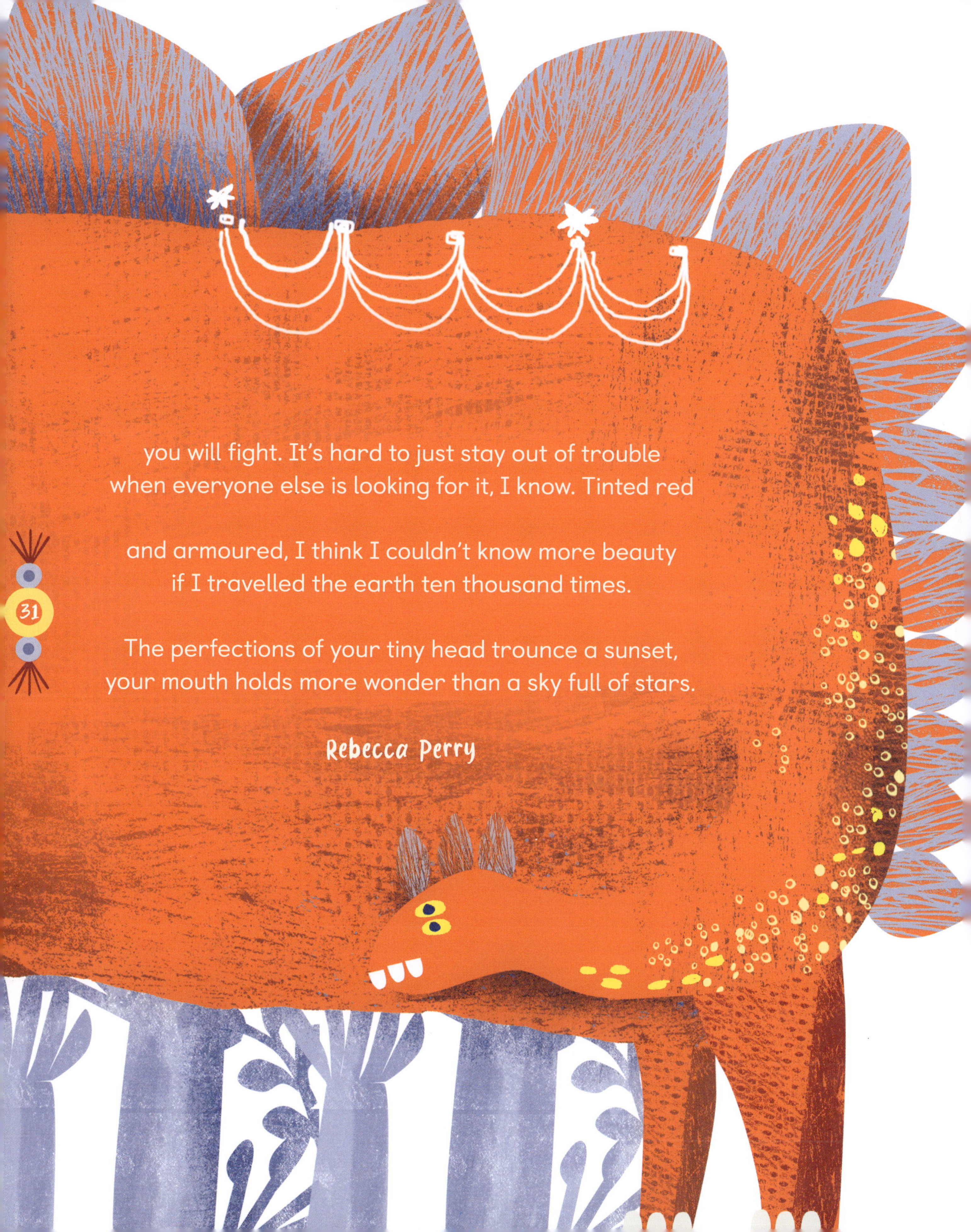

you will fight. It's hard to just stay out of trouble
when everyone else is looking for it, I know. Tinted red

and armoured, I think I couldn't know more beauty
if I travelled the earth ten thousand times.

The perfections of your tiny head trounce a sunset,
your mouth holds more wonder than a sky full of stars.

Rebecca Perry

A Year Well Lived-in

I laid down in the long grass
for just five minutes
but when I woke, found I had become inclined to build.

Foundations came easily – a steady breeze made for a sturdy frame
and heavy autumn storm clouds stood still as stone
grouted into walls with the fractals* from a spider's web.

The floorboards I grew myself
from the length of a summer's day,
and winter's sharp fingers knitted me rugs to cover them
thicker than brambles.

I picked up enough leaves to tile a bathroom
from under a tree
hit too hard by a storm
(well – she wasn't using them anymore)
and washed them clean with a shower of dandelion seeds
sputtering from the faucet.

Grabbed the biggest, fattest slugs,
the ones that gleam with wet,
spiralled them into light sockets
to fill the room with sluggy glow,
asked them to line up their siblings
to make a thousand fairy lights
strung between each beam.

Wild garlic flowers for the windowsills,
white as frost
and fragrant to boot,
sat at the edges of rooms
filled with furniture, built from the solid promise
of spring's new shoots.

The red of newly fallen leaves
I baked into roofing slates,
and atop the sloping eaves
a sparrow took an earwig's wing for a crest
and played cockerel weathervane for fun.

~

When next I came upon the house,
it had built itself bigger than the sky;
a new mat proudly on its step
welcomed the world across its threshold.

Tom Denbigh

*fractal – fractals are never-ending
patterns often found in nature –
like the ends of snowflakes or
the tiny leaves on a fern.

Mountain Gorilla

My fur
is made of brushed lava
from the volcanoes
of Rwanda.
See the ash
on my grandfather's
silver back?
My head:
top of a mountain.
My shoulders:
mountain bluffs.

Earthquake?
That is my father
thumping the ground.
Thunder?
That is my uncle
beating his chest.
Black hail?
Oh, that is my mother
spitting papaya seeds!

Janet Wong

Seamstress

Each night I pull threads of birds
shake them loose; unpick the sky's

dappled husks of thrush and wren
mulberry silk from blackbird eyes

unlacing swathed loops of swifts
tangled ropes of swallows' flight

I wind wet weather onto spools
collect the crystal beads of rain

unknot sleet, smooth soft snow
roll rainbows onto coloured skeins.

Lastly, smoggy chimney smoke
chalky trails from tails of planes.

I clean and press, sew, repair
bring out sky's box; put away

strips of darkness; unpinned stars
fraying shadows, darned in grey.

Then I card, spin; weave again
and sit up till dawn, stitching day.

Sue Hardy-Dawson

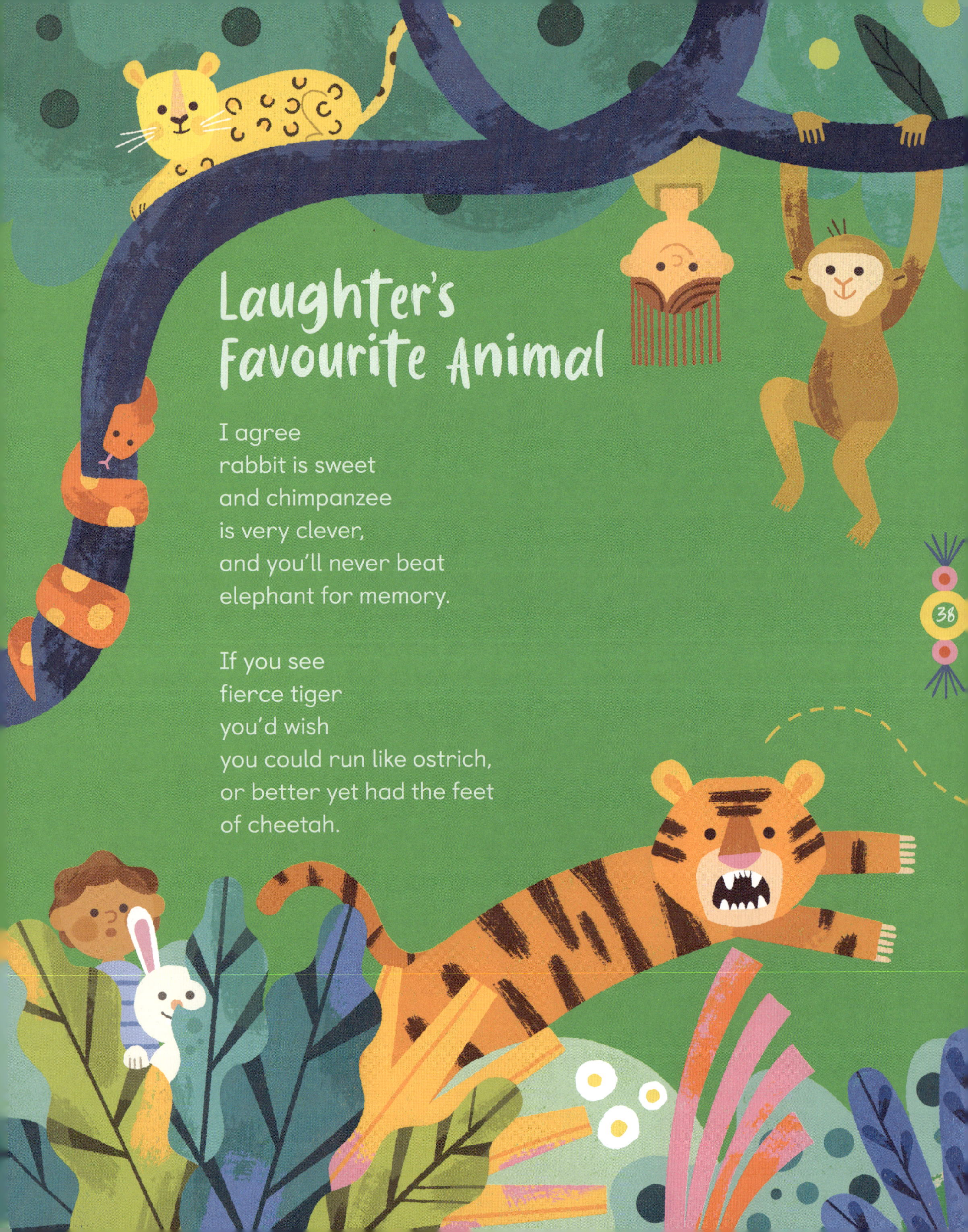

Laughter's Favourite Animal

I agree
rabbit is sweet
and chimpanzee
is very clever,
and you'll never beat
elephant for memory.

If you see
fierce tiger
you'd wish
you could run like ostrich,
or better yet had the feet
of cheetah.

Sure, parrot could chatter,
snake could change skin,
and for a pet
some would pick hamster.
For creepy-crawly feet
you might place a bet
on spider to win.

But alligator
has that special something.
Teeth that seem to laugh.
Teeth that seem to grin.

John Agard

Nature Nurtures

Let me walk in forests,
and climb up all the trees;
let me walk in fields,
and lean into the breeze.

Let me haul the ivy down
from every ruined wall,
and wrap myself in ropes of it,
and never move at all.

Let me lean into an oak
and promise it my heart,
joining with the living wood,
and never let us part.

Let me reach my hand out
where the river waters flow,
clear and cold and swift as wind
and made of melted snow.

Let me become part of this –
the Earth and all that's done;
let me join with root and branch
and stream and stem and Sun.

Let me make my promises
to stone and dirt and tree,
to give myself to all these things
that made humanity.

Jay Hulme

Biographies

Margarita Engle

Margarita Engle is the Cuban-American author of many verse novels, memoirs and picture books, including *The Surrender Tree*, *Enchanted Air* and *Dancing Hands*. Awards include a Newbery Honor, a Pura Belpré and a Golden Kite, among others. Margarita served as the 2017–2019 Young People's Poet Laureate.

Photo credit: Marshall W. Johnson

Diana Hendry

Diana Hendry grew up by the sea on the Wirral peninsula. She's published six collections of poetry and is the author of more than forty books for children – *Harvey Angell* won a Whitbread Award and her young adult novel, *The Seeing*, was shortlisted for a Costa Book Award. She lives in Edinburgh.

Grace Nichols

Grace Nichols was born and educated in Guyana. She has been living in Britain since 1977 and since then has written many award-winning books for adults and children. She has also edited anthologies and won a CLPE Poetry Award. In 2022, Grace was awarded the Queen's Gold Medal for Poetry.

Robert Macfarlane

Robert Macfarlane is a British author and academic who writes for adults and children. His bestseller *The Lost Words* and its sequel *The Lost Spells* were created in partnership with artist Jackie Morris and celebrate the natural world.

Photo credit: Alex Turner

Ruth Awolola

Ruth Awolola is a British-born Nigerian Jamaican poet, workshop facilitator and youth worker. She has been performing poetry since 2015 and was a winner of the national youth slam, SLAMbassadors UK. She has contributed to numerous anthologies including *Rising Stars: New Young Voices in Poetry*.

Naomi Shihab Nye

Palestinian-American poet Naomi Shihab Nye has written books for adults and children, including *Sitti's Secrets* and *Habibi* which both won the Jane Addams Children's Book Award. She was the 2019–2022 Poetry Foundation's Young People's Poet Laureate and received the Ivan Sandrof Lifetime Achievement Award from the National Book Critics Circle in 2020.

Zaro Weil

Zaro Weil won the 2020 CLiPPA for her poetry book *Cherry Moon*. As well as a poet, she has been a dancer, theatre director, actress, playwright, educator and quilt collector to name a few. She now lives in France with a menagerie of animals.

Rachel Plummer

Rachel Plummer is a poet based in Edinburgh. They were a Troubadour International Poetry Prize winner in 2014. Their debut children's poetry collection, *Wain*, is based around LGBT retellings of traditional Scottish myths.

Joyce Sidman

Joyce Sidman is the author of many award-winning children's poetry books. She has also received the NCTE Award for Excellence in Poetry for Children for her body of work. In her home state of Minnesota, USA, she teaches poetry writing to children and walks through the woods with her dog Watson.

Carol Ann Duffy

Carol Ann Duffy is a highly acclaimed and award-winning poet and playwright. She was the first ever female Poet Laureate and held the post from 2009–2019. She is a professor of contemporary poetry at Manchester Metropolitan University and was appointed a DBE in 2015 for services to poetry.

Jack Prelutsky

Jack Prelutsky was the USA's first Children's Poet Laureate. He has filled more than fifty books of verse with his inventive wordplay, including the US bestsellers *Scranimals* and *The New Kid on the Block*. He lives in Washington State. You can visit him online at www.jackprelutsky.com.

Photo credit: Skip Kerr

Mary Ann Hoberman

Mary Ann Hoberman is an American poet and a former Children's Poet Laureate (2008–2011). She is the critically acclaimed author of over forty books for children and has received an Award for Excellence in Poetry for Children, given by the National Council of Teachers of English.

Nikki Giovanni

Nikki Giovanni is an American poet, commentator, activist and educator. She is the author of numerous children's books and poetry collections. Nikki has won many awards and has been nominated for a Grammy. She is a University Distinguished Professor at Virginia Tech.

Jan Dean

Jan Dean is a children's poet with two collections and work in over a hundred anthologies. Jan comes from North West England and now lives in the South West, having slipped down the map.

Rebecca Perry

London-born poet Rebecca Perry has published several poetry pamphlets for adults. Her first book-length collection *Beauty/Beauty* won the Michael Murphy Memorial Prize in 2017 and was shortlisted for numerous other awards.

Tom Denbigh

Tom Denbigh is a poet who lives in Bristol with his dog and boyfriend (listed in order of importance). When he's not eating too much raw garlic, he writes sensible poems about climate change and very silly poems about storytelling.

Photo credit: Colin Potsig

Janet Wong

Janet Wong is an American poet and children's author of over 30 titles. She is the co-publisher of Pomelo Books and the winner of the 2021 NCTE Award for Excellence in Poetry for Children, a prestigious lifetime achievement award.

Photo credit: Emily Vardell

Sue Hardy-Dawson

Sue Hardy-Dawson is a Yorkshire-born poet who has worked with children for 20 years. She is dyslexic and eager to encourage reluctant readers and writers. Her first solo poetry collection *Where Zebras Go* was shortlisted for the CLiPPA in 2018.

John Agard

John Agard was born in Guyana and now lives in the UK. He has published poetry books for adults and children alike and won numerous awards including the BookTrust Lifetime Achievement Award, the CLPE Poetry Award, the Paul Hamlyn Award for Poetry and Queen's Gold Medal for Poetry.

Jay Hulme

Jay Hulme is an award-winning transgender performance poet, speaker and educator. Jay teaches in schools and consults with groups on the importance of diversity and transgender inclusion in literature and the media.

Annalise Barber

A resident of Columbus, Ohio, Annalise Barber illustrates for children and those who are young at heart. She experiments with sinuous shapes, playful narratives and watercolour media. With a paintbrush in her hand, Annalise illustrates to inspire and empower children.

Mariana Roldán

Mariana Roldán is an illustrator based in Mexico. She loves to dance and draw. These activities are how she expresses the feelings that live inside her and how she shares with others the history of the world we live in.

Masha Manapov

Masha Manapov is an award-winning illustrator, author and image-maker. Born in Baku and raised in Tel Aviv, she is currently working from her London-based studio on commissioned projects worldwide.

Nabila Adani

Nabila Adani lives in Jakarta, Indonesia, and enjoys illustrating different world cultures. She briefly worked as a product designer before moving to the United States to study children's book illustration. Now, living back in Jakarta, she enjoys illustrating and telling stories for children worldwide.

Copyright and Acknowledgements

LITTLE TIGER
An imprint of Little Tiger Press Limited
1 Coda Studios, 189 Munster Road, London SW6 6AW
www.littletiger.co.uk
Imported into the EEA by Penguin Random House Ireland,
Morrison Chambers, 32 Nassau Street, Dublin D02 YH68
www.littletigerpress.com
First published in Great Britain 2023 • This edition published 2026

A CIP catalogue record for this book is available from the British Library

ISBN: 978-1-83891-980-1
CPB/2700/3252/0326
2 4 6 8 10 9 7 5 3 1

This book includes poetry written in British and American English. Though the differences are small, we've chosen to keep all writing in its original dialect. The messages in each poem are for everyone but they are also rooted in the places they were dreamt up and written. We wanted to reflect this.